Abide As That

Ramana Maharshi &
The Song of Ribhu

Abide As That

Ramana Maharshi &
The Song of Ribhu

Jason Brett Serle

MANTRA
BOOKS

Winchester, UK
Washington, USA

JOHN HUNT PUBLISHING

First published by Mantra Books, 2019
Mantra Books is an imprint of John Hunt Publishing Ltd., 3 East St., Alresford,
Hampshire SO24 9EE, UK
office@jhpbooks.com
www.johnhuntpublishing.com
www.mantra-books.net

For distributor details and how to order please visit the 'Ordering' section on our website.

Text copyright: Jason Brett Serle 2018

ISBN: 978 1 78904 234 4
978 1 78904 235 1 (ebook)
Library of Congress Control Number: 2018957143

A CIP catalogue record for this book is available from the British Library.

Design: Stuart Davies

UK: Printed and bound by CPI Group (UK) Ltd, Croydon, CR0 4YY
US: Printed and bound by Thomson-Shore, 7300 West Joy Road, Dexter, MI 48130

We operate a distinctive and ethical publishing philosophy in
all areas of our business, from our global network of authors to
production and worldwide distribution.

Contents

Introduction

Ramana's Ribhu Gita

In 1898, shortly after his awakening, Ramana Maharshi was given a copy of the *Ribhu Gita* by his first attendant, Palaniswami. Quick to recognise that its words were a faithful reflection of the state in which he now found himself naturally abiding in, he praised the text highly and, for the rest of his life, found it to be a valuable tool in teaching and a great aid in turning his devotees back towards the ultimate consideration.

He said of this event some years later:

"I had read no books other than Periapuranam, my Bible lessons and bits of Tayumanavar or Tevaram. My notion of God (or Iswara as I called the Infinite but Personal Deity) was similar to that found in the Puranas. I had not heard then of Brahman, samsara, etc. I had no idea that there was an Essence or Impersonal Real underlying everything, and that myself and Iswara were both identical with it. At Tiruvannamalai, as I listened to Ribhu Gita and other works, I picked up these facts and discovered that these books were analysing and naming what I had previously felt intuitively without analysis and name."

The book he was given was a translation into Tamil from Sanskrit, that was considered by many to surpass the original. It was certainly Bhagavan's preferred version and it was often chanted, discussed, and read in his company; most often in the evening, sometimes for hours at a stretch. Occasionally, the readings would last the whole night. After one such marathon and as a testimony to its power, Bhagavan remarked, "These readings from the Ribhu Gita are as good as samadhi."

Recommended to aspirants as a powerful aid to their spiritual development, he would at times present a copy to a devotee to read. On one such occasion, the book was politely declined on the grounds that it was not understood. "It doesn't matter that you do not understand it," he replied, "it will still be of benefit to you."

According to one of his most intimate devotees, Annamalai Swami, "Bhagavan often said that we should read and study the Ribhu Gita regularly. In the Ribhu Gita it is said, 'That wilful consideration "I am not the body, I am not the mind, I am Supreme Being, I am everything" is to be repeated again and again until this becomes the natural state.'"

Later in his life, he would speak of the *Ashtavakra Gita* and the *Ribhu Gita* as being the two highest, most sublime expressions of the true nature of the Self and he is even reported to have said on occasion that by mere repetition of these texts, one could pass into the natural enlightened state.

The version that follows is a selection, made by Bhagavan Sri Ramana Maharshi himself, of 45 verses that capture and communicate the very essence of the enlightened disposition as put forth in the *Ribhu Gita*. A second selection he made of only six verses has also been included.

The Song of Ribhu

The *Ribhu Gita* or *Song of Ribhu* is an ancient Indian spiritual text that is a small portion of a much larger body of writing; an epic poem dedicated to Siva called the *Siva Rahasya*.

The complete text deals with religious observances, spiritual instruction, places of pilgrimage, holy rivers and so forth but in the sixth part of this twelve part work of some 10,000 verses, on the slope of Mount Kedara in the Himalayas, a dialogue takes place between the sage Ribhu and his disciple, Nidagha, in much the same manner as is found in the Upanishads. Indeed, other dialogues between Ribhu and Nidagha are to be found throughout the Upanishads and so it is generally thought that the *Ribhu Gita* originated during this same period, some 2,500 years ago.

And just as its more famous sibling, the *Bhagavad Gita*, is only a small chapter from the *Mahabharata* but yet manages to embody the spiritual essence of the whole epic, so too does the *Ribhu Gita* give to us the distilled spiritual nectar of the *Siva Rahasya.*

Like the *Bhagavad Gita,* it is a dialogue between an Enlightened One and his disciple, however, this time, instead of Krishna, an avatar of Vishnu, we hear Ribhu, who scriptures tell us was a direct disciple of Siva himself.

Indeed, just as the *Bhagavad Gita* represents the highest most exalted declaration of Vishnu, the *Ribhu Gita* represents the purest, most sublime declaration of Siva.

I make these comparisons perhaps only because it would be wise to note that the two of them seem to be in perfect agreement as to the true nature of Reality.

Indeed, in these transcendent realms wherein we approach the perfection of Wisdom, we will find no argument.

The Song of Ribhu belongs firmly in this category; an uncompromising yet tender expression of pure Advaita or non-duality and a shining example of the Ultimate Understanding as transmitted through the guise of Indian Vedanta.

This Supreme Doctrine has been revealed to mankind time and time again through the ages, through the prophets, oracles, saints and sages of every tradition.

It has been alluded to, hinted at, pointed towards, written, spoken, and sung about, but rarely has it been presented with such profound simplicity and such penetrating spiritual force as can be found in *The Song of Ribhu.* Read it well and abide as That.

A Story of Ribhu & Nidagha

As told by Sri Ramana Maharshi

Although Ribhu taught his disciple the Supreme Truth of the One Absolute Reality without a second, Nidagha, in spite of his erudition and understanding, did not get sufficient conviction to adopt and follow the path of Self-knowledge but settled down in his native town to lead a life devoted to the observance of ceremonial religion.

But the Sage loved his disciple as deeply as the latter venerated his Master. In spite of his age, Ribhu would himself go to his disciple in the town just to see how far the latter had outgrown his ritualism. At times the Sage went in disguise so that he might observe how Nidagha would act when he did not know that he was being observed by his Master.

On one such occasion Ribhu, who had put on the disguise of a village rustic, found Nidagha intently watching a royal procession. Unrecognised by the town dweller Nidagha, the village rustic enquired what the bustle was all about, and was told that the king was going in procession.

"Oh! It is the king. He goes in procession! But where is he?" asked the rustic.

"There, on the elephant," said Nidagha.

"You say the king is on the elephant. Yes, I see the two," said the rustic, "but which is the king and which is the elephant?"

"What!" exclaimed Nidagha. "You see the two, but do not know that the man above is the king, and the animal below is the elephant? Where is the use of talking to a man like you?"

"Pray, be not impatient with an ignorant man like me," begged the rustic. "But you said 'above' and 'below', what do they mean?"

Nidagha could stand it no more. "You see the king and the elephant, the one above and the other below. Yet you want to know what is meant by 'above' and 'below'?" burst out Nidagha. "If things seen and words spoken can convey so little to you, action alone can teach you. Bend forward, and you will know it all too well."

The rustic did as he was told. Nidagha got on his shoulders and said, "Know it now. I am above as the king, you are below as the elephant. Is that clear enough?"

"No, not yet," was the rustic's quiet reply. "You say you are above like the king, and I am below like the elephant. The 'king', the 'elephant', 'above' and 'below', so far it is clear. But pray, tell me what you mean by 'I' and 'you'?"

When Nidagha was thus confronted all of a sudden with the mighty problem of defining the 'you' apart from the 'I', light dawned on his mind. At once he jumped down and fell at his Master's feet saying: "Who else but my venerable Master, Ribhu, could have thus drawn my mind from duality and the superficialities of physical existence to the true Being of the Self? Oh! Benign Master! I crave thy blessings!"

A Note on the Translation

The original Sanskrit version of the *Ribhu Gita* was translated into Tamil in the late 1800s by Bhikshu Sastrigal, also known as Ulagantha Swamigal. The first English translation from the Tamil was originally published in *The Mountain Path*, Volume 9, Numbers 1 and 2 in 1972.

The translation that follows has been revised and edited, and many of the terms that remained untranslated in the original English have been rendered into their English equivalents.

The reasons for this are twofold. The *Ribhu Gita* is not a complex technical text, in fact, it is quite the opposite. The untranslated terms, therefore, were not technical and nor were they unique to Indian thought but were rather universal philosophical terms such as *jnana* or 'Self-knowledge', *jiva*, 'separate soul' or *Atman*, the 'Self', and I found that without exception, they could be easily rendered into English, using at most, a handful of words.

The second reason is that it allows the average English-speaking reader to more readily immerse themselves in the substance of the text rather than being distracted, if only mildly, by terms that require a secondary consideration as to their meaning.

I have also taken this liberty in revising the questions and answers that follow. I can only hope that it serves to further the cause of Self-knowledge as is my only intention. Any faults or mistakes are purely my own.

May Ribhu and Bhagavan forgive any transgressions!

The Essence of the Ribhu Gita

A selection of 6 verses by Sri Ramana Maharshi

1.

The concept 'I-am-the-body' is the sentient inner organ, the mind. It is also the illusory identification with birth and death. It is the source of all groundless fears. If there is no trace of it at all, everything will be found to be Supreme Spirit.

2.

The concept 'I-am-the-body' is the primal ignorance. It is known as the firm knot of the heart. It gives rise to the concepts of existence and non-existence. If there is no trace of it at all, everything will be found to be Supreme Spirit.

3.

The separate soul is a concept. God, the world, the mind, desires, action, sorrow, and all other things are all concepts.

4.

Abiding without concepts is the undifferentiated state. It is inherence in the Supreme Being. It is Wisdom. It is Liberation. It is the natural state. It is the Absolute. It is the Supreme Formless Spirit. If there is no concept at all, everything will be found to be Supreme Spirit.

5.

The body is only a concept. Hearing, reasoning and contemplating are concepts. Self-enquiry is a concept. All other things are also concepts. Concepts give rise to the world, separate souls, and God. There is nothing whatever except concepts. Everything is in truth, Supreme Spirit.

6.

The mind is unreal. It is like a magic show. It is like the son of a barren woman. It is absolutely non-existent. Since there is no mind, there are no concepts, no Sage, no seeker, no world, no separate soul. All concepts are really Supreme Spirit.

The Song of Ribhu

A selection of 45 verses by Sri Ramana Maharshi

Chapter 26 – Verses 1–45

1

I shall now expound to you the method of inhering in the All-inclusive and undifferentiated Reality. This teaching is secret and difficult to understand even with the help of the scriptures. Even divine beings and sages who hold it dear acquire it only with great difficulty. Follow what I say and, inhering in Reality, be happy.

2

My son! Realised sages say that absolute inherence in Reality means becoming one with the immutable, tranquil, non-dual Absolute which is Being-Consciousness-Beatitude and the Self of all, and making the wandering mind one with it like the proverbial milk and water, absolutely free from all concepts.

3

When one scrutinises this variety of manifestation, one
realises that it does not really exist and that everything is
the undifferentiated Absolute which is not different from the
Self. Let this knowledge become firm in you through constant
practice. Then, discarding everything, become One with the
Absolute and, remaining as that, be happy.

4

Abide as That which does not, when scrutinised, show any duality in the form of these various objects or the least trace of cause and effect, That in which, when the mind is absorbed in It, there is no fear of duality at all – and be always happy, unshakable and free from the fear arising from duality.

5

Abide as That in which there are neither thoughts nor fancies, neither peace nor self-control, neither the mind nor the intellect, neither confusion nor certainty, neither being nor non-being, and no perception of duality – and be always happy, unshakable and absolutely free from the fear arising from duality.

6

Abide as That in which there is neither any defect nor good quality, neither pleasure nor pain, neither thought nor silence, neither misery nor the desire to escape misery, no 'I-am-the-body' idea, no objects of perception whatsoever – and be always happy, free from all traces of thought.

7

Abide as That in which there is no work, physical, mental, verbal, or of any other kind, neither sin nor virtue, neither attachment nor its consequences – and be always happy, free from all traces of thought.

8

Abide as That in which there are neither thoughts nor a thinker, neither the arising nor the preservation nor the dissolution of the world, nothing whatsoever at any time – and be always happy, free from all traces of thought.

9

Abide as That in which there is neither the self-limiting power of Illusion nor its effects, neither knowledge nor ignorance, neither separate soul nor personal deity, neither being nor non-being, neither world nor God – and be always happy, free from all traces of thought.

10

Abide as That in which there are no gods and their worship, none of the three Divine Powers of Creation, Preservation and Destruction nor meditation on them, no Supreme God nor meditation on Him – and be always happy, without the least trace of thought.

11

Abide as That in which there is neither the consequence of past action nor searching devotion nor self-knowledge, no fruit of action to be enjoyed, no supreme state separate from it, no means of attainment or object to be attained and be always happy, free from all traces of thought.

12

Abide as That in which there is neither body nor senses nor vital forces, neither mind nor intellect nor fancy, neither ego nor ignorance, nor anyone who identifies himself with them, neither the macrocosm nor the microcosm, and be always happy, free from all traces of thought.

13

Abide as That in which there is neither desire nor anger, neither greed nor delusion, neither ill-will nor pride, no impurities of mind and no false notions of bondage and liberation – and be always happy, free from all traces of thought.

14

Abide as That in which there is no beginning or end, no top or bottom or middle, no holy place or god, no gifts or pious acts, no time or space, no objects of perception – and be always happy, free from all traces of thought.

15

Abide as That in which there is no discrimination between the real and the unreal, no absence of desire, no possession of virtues, no yearning for liberation, no competent Sage or seeker, no steady knowledge, no realised stage, no liberation in life or death, nothing whatsoever at any time – and be always happy free from all traces of thought.

16

Abide as That in which there are no scriptures or sacred books, no one who thinks, no objection or answer to it, no theory to be established, no theory to be rejected, nothing other than One Self – and be always happy, free from the least trace of thought.

17

Abide as That in which there is no debate, no success or failure, no word or its meaning, no speech, no difference between the soul and the Supreme Being, none of the manifold causes and consequences – and be always happy, without the least trace of thought.

18

Abide as That in which there is no need for learning, reflecting and practising, no meditation to be practised, nothing different, nothing the same, and no internal contradictions, no words or their meanings – and be always happy, free from the least trace of thought.

19

Abide as That in which there are no fears of hell, no joys of heaven, no worlds of the Creator God or the other Gods, or any object to be gained from them, no other world, no universe of any kind – and be always happy, without the least trace of thought.

20

Abide as That in which there is nothing of the elements nor even an iota of their derivatives, no sense of 'I' or 'mind', no fantasies of the mind, no blemish of attachment, no concept whatsoever – and be always happy, without the least trace of thought.

21

Abide as That in which there are none of the three kinds of
bodies (gross, subtle and causal), none of the three kinds of
states (waking, dreaming and sleeping), none of the three kinds
of souls (those who are fully prepared to advance spiritually,
those who are not fully prepared, and those who are not
prepared at all), none of the three kinds of afflictions (those
of the body, those caused by the elements, and those caused
by fate), none of the five kinds of sheaths (physical, vital,
emotional, intellectual, and blissful), no one to identify himself
with them – and be always happy, without the least trace of
thought.

22

Abide as That in which there is no sentient object, no power to hide Reality, no difference of any kind, no power of projecting unreal objects, no power of any other kind, no false notion about the world – and be always happy, without the least trace of thought.

23

Abide as That in which there are no sense organs or anyone to use them, That in which transcendent bliss is experienced, That which is absolutely immediate, That which by realising and attaining, one becomes immortal, That which, by becoming, one does not return to this cycle of births and deaths – and be always happy, without the least trace of thought.

24

Abide as That, on realising and experiencing the bliss of which, all joys appear to be the joys of That, That which, when clearly known to be oneself, shows there is nothing apart from oneself, and, knowing which, all kinds of separate souls become liberated – and be always happy, without the least trace of thought.

25

Abide as That, on realising which to be oneself, there is nothing else to be known, everything becomes already known and every purpose accomplished – and be always happy, without the least trace of thought.

26

Abide as That which is attained easily when one is convinced that one is not different from the Absolute, That which results, when the conviction becomes firm, in the experience of the supreme bliss of the Absolute, That which produces a sense of incomparable and complete satisfaction when the mind is absorbed in It – and be always happy, without the least trace of thought.

27

Abide as That which leads to the complete cessation of misery when the mind is absorbed in It, and the extinction of all ideas of 'I', 'you' and 'it', and the disappearance of all differences – and be always happy, without the least trace of thought.

28

Abide as That in which, when the mind is absorbed in It, one remains without a second, nothing other than oneself is seen to exist and incomparable bliss is experienced – and be always happy, without the least trace of thought.

29

Abide as That which is undifferentiated Being, undifferentiated Consciousness, undifferentiated Beatitude, absolutely non-dual, the undifferentiated Absolute – and with the firm conviction that you are That, be always happy.

30

Abide as That which is 'I' as well as 'you' as well as
everyone else, is the basis of all, is One without anything else
whatsoever, is extremely pure, the undifferentiated Whole
– and with the firm conviction that you are That, be always
happy.

31

Abide as That in which there are no concepts or anything else whatsoever, the ego ceases to exist, all desires disappear, the mind becomes extinct and all confusions come to an end – and with the firm conviction that you are That, be always happy.

32

Abide as That in which there is no awareness of the body, no perception of objects, That in which the mind is dead, the soul becomes one with Reality, thoughts are dissolved and even one's convictions no longer hold – and with the firm conviction that you are That, be always happy.

33

Abide as That which is the Supreme Reality, in which there is no longer any concentration or meditation, or ignorance or knowledge, or activities of any kind – and with the firm conviction that you are That, be always happy.

34

Abide as That in which, when one is completely merged with It, one experiences pure bliss, never experiences misery, sees nothing, does not take birth again, never thinks oneself to be a separate individual, becomes the Supreme Being and with the conviction that you are That, be always happy.

35

Abide as That which is truly the Absolute, the Formless Unmanifest, the absolutely pure Being, the Supreme State, Absolute Consciousness, the Supreme Truth – and with the conviction that you are That, be always happy.

36

Abide as That which is the absolutely pure Supreme Being, absolute Bliss, the supremely subtle Spirit, the Self-Effulgent, non-dual and undifferentiated One – and with the conviction that you are That, be always happy.

37

Abide as That which is absolute Truth, supreme Tranquillity,
eternal Being, absolutely attributeless, the Self, the absolutely
undifferentiated Supreme Being – and with the conviction that
you are That, be always happy.

38

Abide as That which is everything from the experiential point of view and nothing from the absolute point of view, Being-Consciousness-Beatitude, always tranquil, with nothing separate from It, the self-existent Being – and with the conviction that you are That, be always happy.

39

I have thus, O Nidagha, clearly explained to you the state of being One with the Supreme Being. By constantly thinking that you are the undifferentiated Supreme Being, you can attain that state and enjoy constant bliss. Thereafter, having become the Divine Absolute Reality, you will never experience the misery of birth and death.

40

Everything is the Supreme Spirit, which is Being-Consciousness-Beatitude, and I am That. By constantly cultivating this pure thought, get rid of impure thoughts. Then, my son, discarding even that thought and always inhering in the State of Fullness, you will become the non-dual and undifferentiated Supreme Being and attain liberation.

41

Pure and impure thoughts are a feature of the mind. There are no wandering thoughts in the Supreme Being. Therefore, abide as That and, free from the pure and impure thoughts of the mind, remain still like a stone or a log of wood. You will then be always happy.

42

By constantly thinking of the undifferentiated Supreme Being and forgetting thereby all thoughts, including the thought of the Supreme Being, you will become the all-comprehensive Supreme Being. Even a great sinner who hears and understands this teaching will get rid of all his sins and become the undifferentiated Supreme Being.

43

The endless scriptures have already prescribed meditation for attaining purity of mind. The nature of this immaculate State has been expounded by me in order that those who have become pure in mind may easily attain liberation and, realising that they are absolute and boundless Bliss, remain still like a stone in the undifferentiated and all-comprehensive Formless Unmanifest.

44

Therefore, attaining purity of mind by constantly thinking that everything that is known is Supreme Being and that Supreme Being is oneself, and thereafter abiding in the state of complete identity with the Absolute Reality, liberation can be attained here and now. I have spoken the truth. In this manner, Sage Ribhu expounded the true and natural state of being to Nidagha.

45

When one is convinced that one is always That which is
Being-Consciousness-Beatitude and abides as That in a state
of complete identity, one casts off the unreal bondage of
birth and death and attains liberation. This is the significance
of the highly blissful mood and dance of our Supreme and
undifferentiated God.

In His Own Words

Elucidations on the themes, taken from conversations between Sri Ramana Maharshi and devotees

All is Supreme Spirit

Q. All are said to be Supreme Spirit.

A. Yes, they are but so long as you think that they are apart they are to be avoided. If on the other hand they are found to be Self there is no need to say 'all'. For all that exists is only Supreme Spirit. There is nothing besides Supreme Spirit.

Q. The Ribhu Gita speaks of so many objects as unreal, adding at the end that they are all Supreme Spirit and thus real.

A. Yes. When you see them as so many they are unreal, whereas when you see them as Supreme Spirit they are real, deriving their reality from their substratum, Supreme Spirit.

Who Am I?

Q. Who am I? How is it to be found?

A. Ask yourself the question. The body and its functions are not 'I'. Going deeper, the mind and its functions are not 'I'. This step leads to the question, "From where do these thoughts arise?" The thoughts are spontaneous, superficial or analytical. They operate in the intellect. Then, who is aware of them? The existence of thoughts, their clear conceptions and their operations become evident to the individual. The analysis leads to the conclusion that the individuality of the person is operative as the perceiver of the existence of thoughts and of their sequence. This individuality is the ego, or as people say 'I'. The intellect is only a sheath of 'I' and not the 'I' itself.

Enquiring further the questions arise, "Who is this 'I'? From where does it come?" 'I' was not aware in sleep. Simultaneously with its rise, sleep changes to dream or wakefulness. But I am not concerned with dream just now. Who am I now, in the wakeful state? If I originated from sleep, then the 'I' was covered up with ignorance. Such an ignorant 'I' cannot be what the scriptures say or the wise ones affirm.

'I' am beyond even 'Sleep'; 'I' must be now and here and what I was all along in sleep and dreams also, without the qualities of such states. 'I' must, therefore, be the unqualified substratum underlying these three states.

'I' is, in brief, beyond the five sheaths. Next, the residuum left over after discarding all that is not-self is the Self; Being-Consciousness-Beatitude.

Q. How is that Self to be known or realised?

A. Transcend the present plane of relativity. A separate self will appear to know something apart from itself. That is, the subject is aware of the object. The subject is the seer and the object, the seen. There must be a unity underlying these two, which arises as 'ego'. This ego is of the nature of intelligence whereas, in an insentient object, there is only the absence of intelligence. Therefore the underlying essence is akin to the subject and not the object. Seeking the seer, until all of the seen disappears, the seen will become subtler and subtler until the absolute Seer alone survives. This process is called 'the disappearance of the objective world'.

Q. Why should the objects seen be eliminated? Cannot the Truth be realised even keeping the object as it is?

A. No. Elimination of the seen means elimination of separate identities of the subject and object. The object is unreal. All of the seen, including the ego, is the object. Eliminating the unreal, the Reality survives. When a rope is mistaken for a snake, it is enough to remove the erroneous perception of the snake for the truth to be revealed. Without such elimination, the truth will not dawn.

Q. When and how is the disappearance of the objective world to be effected?

A. It is complete when the relative subject, namely the mind, is eliminated. The mind is the creator of the subject and the object and is the cause of the dualistic idea. Therefore, it is the cause of the wrong notion of a limited self and the misery consequent on such an erroneous idea.

Q. What is this mind?

A. Mind is one form of manifestation of life. A block of wood or a subtle machine is not called mind. The vital force manifests as life activity and also as the conscious phenomena known as the mind.

Q. What is the relation between mind and object? Is the mind contacting something different from it, viz., the world?

A. The world is 'sensed' in the waking and the dream states or is the object of perception and thought, both being mental activities. If there were no such activities as waking and dreaming thought, there would be no 'perception' or inference of a 'world'. In sleep, there is no such activity and 'objects and world' do not exist for us in sleep. Hence 'reality of the world' may be created by the ego by its act of emergence from sleep, and that reality may be swallowed up or disappear by the soul resuming its nature in sleep. The emergence and disappearance of the world are like the spider producing a gossamer web and then withdrawing it. The spider here underlies all the three states – waking, dreaming, and sleep; such a spider in the person is called the Self, whereas the same with reference to the world (which is considered to issue from the sun) is called Supreme Spirit. He that is in man is the same as He that is in the sun. (Sa yaschayam purushe yaschasavaditye sa ekah.)

While Self or Spirit is unmanifest and inactive, there are no relative doubles; e.g., subject and object, the seer and the seen. If the enquiry into the ultimate cause of manifestation of mind itself is pushed on, mind will be found to be only the manifestation of the Real which is otherwise called the Self or Supreme Spirit. The mind is termed the 'subtle-body', and the soul is the individual soul. The soul is the essence of the growth of individuality; personality is referred to as part of the soul. Thought or mind is said to be its phase, or one of the ways in which the soul manifests itself – the earlier stage or phase of such manifestation being vegetative life. This mind is always seen as being related to, or acting on, some non-mind or matter, and never by itself. Therefore mind and matter coexist.

How to Know the 'I'

Q. How to know the 'I'?

A. The 'I-I' is always there. There is no knowing it. It is not a new knowledge acquired. What is new and not here and now will be evanescent only. The 'I' is always there. There is obstruction to its knowledge and it is called ignorance. Remove the ignorance and knowledge shines forth. In fact, this ignorance or even knowledge is not for the Self. They are only overgrowths to be cleared off. That is why the Self is said to be beyond knowledge and ignorance. It remains as it naturally is – that is all.

Q. But there is no perceptible progress in spite of our attempts.

A. Progress can be spoken of in things to be obtained afresh. Whereas here it is the removal of ignorance and not the acquisition of knowledge. What kind of progress can be expected in the quest for the Self?

Q. How to remove the ignorance?

A. While lying in bed you dream in your sleep that you find yourself in another town. The scene is real to you. Your body remains here on your bed in a room. Can a town enter your room, or could you have left this place and gone elsewhere, leaving the body here? Both are impossible. Therefore your being here and seeing another town are both unreal. They appear real to the mind. The 'I' of the dream soon vanishes, then another 'I' speaks of the dream. This 'I' was not in the dream. Both the 'I's are unreal. There is the substratum of the mind which continues all along, giving rise to so many scenes. An 'I' rises forth with every thought and with its disappearance that 'I' disappears too. Many 'I's are born and die every moment. The subsisting mind is the real trouble.

The World As Supreme Spirit

Q. "The Supreme Spirit is Real. The world is illusion," is the stock phrase of Sri Sankaracharya. Yet others say, "The world is Supreme Spirit." Which is true?

A. Both statements are true. They refer to different stages of development and are spoken from different points of view. The aspirant starts with the definition, that which is real exists always; then he eliminates the world as unreal because it is changing. It cannot be real; 'not this, not this!' The seeker ultimately reaches the Self and there finds unity as the prevailing note. Then, that which was originally rejected as being unreal is found to be a part of the unity. Being absorbed in the Reality, the world also is Real. There is only being in Self-Realisation, and nothing but being. Again Reality is used in a different sense and is applied loosely by some thinkers to objects. They say that the reflected Reality admits of degrees which are named:

(1) Everyday reality – this chair is seen by me and is real.
(2) Illusory reality – the Illusion of a serpent in a coiled rope. The appearance is real to the man who thinks so. This phenomenon appears at a point in time and under certain circumstances.
(3) Ultimate Reality – that which remains the same always and without change.

If Reality be used in the wider sense the world may be said to have the everyday life and illusory degrees. Some, however, deny even the reality of practical life and consider it to be only a projection of the mind. According to them, it is only an illusion.

Know Thy Self

Q. How to realise Self?

A. Whose Self? Find out.

Q. Who am I?

A. Find it yourself.

Q. I do not know.

A. Think. Who is it that says, "I do not know"? What is not known? In that statement, who is the 'I'?

Q. Somebody in me.

A. Who is the somebody? In whom?

Q. Maybe some power.

A. Find it.

Q. How to realise Supreme Spirit?

A. Without knowing the Self why seek to know Supreme Spirit?

Q. The scriptures say Supreme Spirit pervades all and me too.

A. Find the 'I' in me and then there will be time to think of Supreme Spirit.

Q. Why was I born?

A. Who was born? The answer is the same for all of your questions.

Q. Who am I then?

A. (Smiling) Have you come to examine me and ask me? You must say who you are.

Q. In deep sleep the soul leaves the body and remains elsewhere. When it re-enters I awake. Is it so?

A. What is it that leaves the body?

Q. The power, perhaps.

A. Find out the power.

Q. The body is composed of five elements. What are the elements?

M. Without knowing the Self how do you aim to know the elements?

Being-Consciousness-Beatitude

Q. The Supreme Spirit is said to be Being-Consciousness-Beatitude. What does that mean?

A. Yes. That is so. That which is, is only Being. That is called Supreme Spirit. The lustre of Being is Consciousness and its nature is Beatitude. These are not different from Being. All the three together are known as Being-Consciousness-Beatitude.

Q. As the Self is Being and Consciousness, what is the reason for describing it as different from the existent and the non-existent, the sentient and the insentient?

A. Although the Self is Real, as it comprises everything, it does not give room for questions involving duality about its reality or unreality. Therefore it is said to be different from the real and the unreal. Similarly, even though it is Consciousness, since there is nothing for it to know or to make itself known to, it is said to be different from the sentient and the insentient.

Being-Consciousness-Beatitude is said to indicate that the Supreme is not different from Being, not different from Consciousness and not different from Beatitude. Because we are in the phenomenal world we speak of the Self as Being-Consciousness-Beatitude.

Q. In what sense is happiness or Beatitude our real nature?

A. Perfect Beatitude is the Supreme Spirit. Perfect Being is of the Self. That alone exists and is Consciousness. That which is called happiness is only the nature of Self; Self is not other than perfect happiness. That which is called perfect happiness alone exists. Knowing that fact and abiding in the state of Self, enjoy bliss eternally. If a man thinks that his happiness is due to external causes and his possessions, it is reasonable to conclude that his happiness must increase with an increase in possessions and diminish in proportion to their diminution. Therefore if he is devoid of possessions, his happiness should be nil. What is the real experience of man? Does it conform to this view? In deep sleep, man is devoid of possessions, including his own body.

Instead of being unhappy he is quite happy. Everyone desires to sleep soundly. The conclusion is that happiness is inherent in man and is not due to external causes. One must realise the Self in order to open the store of unalloyed happiness.

Self-Realisation

Q. How can I attain Self-realisation?

A. Realisation is nothing to be gained afresh; it is already there. All that is necessary is to get rid of the thought 'I have not realised'. Stillness or peace is realisation. There is no moment when the Self is not. So long as there is doubt or the feeling of non-realisation, the attempt should be made to rid oneself of these thoughts. They are due to the identification of the Self with the not-Self. When the not-Self disappears, the Self alone remains. To make room, it is enough that objects be removed. Room is not brought in from elsewhere.

Q. Since realisation is not possible without the destruction of mental tendencies, how am I to realise that state in which the tendencies are effectively destroyed?

A. You are in that state now.

Q. Does it mean that by holding on to the Self, the mental tendencies should be destroyed as and when they emerge?

A. They will themselves be destroyed if you remain as you are.

Q. How shall I reach the Self?

A. There is no reaching the Self. If Self were to be reached, it would mean that the Self is not here and now and that it is yet to be obtained. What is got afresh will also be lost. So it will be impermanent. What is not permanent is not worth striving for. So I say the Self is not reached. You are the Self, you are already that.

The fact is, you are ignorant of your blissful state. Ignorance supervenes and draws a veil over the pure Self which is bliss. Attempts are directed only to remove this veil of ignorance which is merely wrong knowledge. The wrong knowledge is the false identification of the Self with the body and the mind. This false identification must go, and then the Self alone remains. Therefore realisation is for everyone; realisation makes no difference between the aspirants. This very doubt, whether you can realise, and the notion 'I-have-not-realised' are themselves the obstacles. Be free from these obstacles also.

Q. How long does it take to reach liberation?

A. Liberation is not to be gained in the future. It is there forever, here and now.

Q. I agree, but I do not experience it.

A. The experience is here and now. One cannot deny one's own Self.

Q. That means existence and not happiness.

A. Existence is the same as happiness and happiness is the same as being. The word liberation is so provoking. Why should one seek it? One believes that there is bondage and therefore seeks liberation. But the fact is that there is no bondage but only liberation. Why call it by a name and seek it?

Q. True – but we are ignorant.

A. Only remove ignorance. That is all there is to be done.

The Tenth Man

Q. Is not the realisation of one's Absolute Being something quite unattainable for a layman like me?

A. The realisation of one's Absolute Being is not a knowledge to be acquired, so that acquiring it one may obtain happiness. It is one's ignorant outlook that one should give up. The Self you seek to know is truly yourself. Your supposed ignorance causes you needless grief like that of the ten foolish men who grieved at the loss of the tenth man who was never lost. The ten foolish men in the parable forded a stream and on reaching the other shore wanted to make sure that all of them had in fact safely crossed the stream. One of the ten began to count, but while counting the others left himself out. "I see only nine; sure enough, we have lost one. Who can it be?" he said. "Did you count correctly?" asked another, and did the counting himself. But he too counted only nine. One after the other each of the ten counted only nine, missing himself. "We are only nine," they all agreed, "but who is the missing one?" they asked themselves. Every effort they made to discover the 'missing' individual failed. "Whoever he is that is drowned," said the most sentimental of the ten fools, "we have lost him." So saying he burst into tears, and the others followed suit. Seeing them weeping on the riverbank, a sympathetic wayfarer enquired about the cause. They related what had happened and said that even after counting themselves several times they could find no more than nine. On hearing the story, but seeing all the ten before him, the wayfarer guessed what had happened. In order to make them know for themselves they were really ten, that all of them had survived the crossing, he told them, "Let each of you count for himself but one after the other serially, one, two, three and so on, while I shall give you each a blow so that all of you may be sure of having been included in the count, and included only once. The tenth missing man will then be found."

Hearing this they rejoiced at the prospect of finding their 'lost' comrade and accepted the method suggested by the wayfarer. While the kind wayfarer gave a blow to each of the ten in turn, he that got the blow counted himself aloud. "Ten," said the last man as he got the last blow in his turn. Bewildered they looked at one another, "We are ten," they said with one voice and thanked the wayfarer for having removed their grief. That is the parable. From where was the tenth man brought in? Was he ever lost? By knowing that he had been there all the while, did they learn anything new? The cause of their grief was not the real loss of anyone, it was their own ignorance, or rather, their mere supposition that one of them was lost. Such is the case with you. Truly there is no cause for you to be miserable and unhappy. You yourself impose limitations on your true nature of infinite Being, and then weep that you are but a finite creature. Then you take up this or that spiritual practice to transcend the non-existent limitations. But if your spiritual practice itself assumes the existence of the limitations, how can it help you to transcend them?

Hence I say know that you are really the infinite pure Being, the Self. You are always that Self and nothing but that Self. Therefore, you can never be really ignorant of the Self. Your ignorance is merely an imaginary ignorance, like the ignorance of the ten fools about the lost tenth man. It is this ignorance that caused them grief. Know then that true knowledge does not create a new being for you, it only removes your ignorant ignorance. Bliss is not added to your nature, it is merely revealed as your true natural state, eternal and imperishable. The only way to be rid of your grief is to know and be the Self. How can this be unattainable?

Understanding

Q. However often Bhagavan teaches us, we are not able to understand.

A. People say that they are not able to know the Self that is all pervading. What can I do? Even the smallest child says, "I exist; I do; this is mine." So, everyone understands that the thing 'I' is always existent. It is only when that 'I' is there that there is the feeling that you are the body, he is Venkanna, this is Ramana and so on. To know that the one that is always visible is one's own Self, is it necessary to search with a candle? To say that we do not know the real nature of the Self, which is not different but which is in one's own Self is like saying, "I do not know myself."

Q. But how is one to reach this state?

A. There is no goal to be reached. There is nothing to be attained. You are the Self. You exist always. Nothing more can be predicated of the Self than that it exists. Seeing God or the Self is only being the Self or yourself. Seeing is being. You, being the Self, want to know how to attain the Self. It is something like a man being at Ramanasramam asking how many ways there are to reach Ramanasramam and which is the best way for him. All that is required of you is to give up the thought that you are this body and to give up all thoughts of the external things or the not-Self.

Q. What is the ego-self? How is it related to the real Self?

A. The ego-self appears and disappears and is transitory, whereas the real Self is permanent. Though you are actually the true Self you wrongly identify the real Self with the ego-self.

Q. How does the mistake come about?

A. See if it has come about.

Q. One has to sublimate the ego-self into the true Self.

A. The ego-self does not exist at all.

Q. Why does it give us trouble?

A. To whom is the trouble? The trouble also is imagined. Trouble and pleasure are only for the ego.

Q. Why is the world so wrapped up in ignorance?

A. Take care of yourself. Let the world take care of itself. See your Self. If you are the body there is the gross world also. If you are Spirit, all is Spirit alone.

Q. It will hold good for the individual, but what of the rest?

A. Do it first and then see if the question arises afterwards.

Q. Is there ignorance?

A. For whom is it?

Q. For the ego-self.

A. Yes, for the ego. Remove the ego and ignorance is gone. Look for it, the ego vanishes and the real Self alone remains. The ego professing ignorance is not to be seen. There is no ignorance in Reality. All scriptures are meant to banish the existence of ignorance.

Q. How did the ego arise?

A. Ego is not. Otherwise, do you admit of two selves? How

can there be ignorance in the absence of the ego? If you begin to enquire, the ignorance, which is already non-existent, will be found not to be, or you will say it has fled away. Ignorance pertains to the ego. Why do you think of the ego and also suffer? What is ignorance again? It is that which is non-existent. However, the worldly life requires the hypothesis of ignorance. Ignorance is only our ignorance and nothing more. It is ignorance or forgetfulness of the Self. Can there be darkness before the sun? Similarly, can there be ignorance before the self-evident and self-luminous Self? If you know the Self there will be no darkness, no ignorance and no misery. It is the mind which feels the trouble and the misery. Darkness never comes nor goes. See the sun there is no darkness. Similarly, see the Self and ignorance will be found not to exist.

Q. How has the unreal come? Can the unreal spring from the real?

A. See if it has sprung. There is no such thing as the unreal, from another standpoint. The Self alone exists. When you try to trace the ego, which is the basis of the perception of the world and everything else, you find the ego does not exist at all and neither does all this creation that you see.

The Nature of the Sage

Q. What is the difference between the bound man and the liberated one?

A. The ordinary man lives in the brain unaware of himself in the Heart. The sage lives in the Heart. When he moves about and deals with men and things, he knows that what he sees is not separate from the one Supreme Reality which he realised in the Heart as his own Self, the Real.

Q. What about the ordinary man?

A. I have just said that he sees things outside himself. He is separate from the world, from his own deeper truth, from the truth that supports him and what he sees. The man who has realised the Supreme Truth of his own existence realises that it is the one Supreme Reality that is there behind him, behind the world. In fact, he is aware of the One, as the Real, the Self in all selves, in all things, eternal and immutable, in all that is impermanent and mutable.

Q. What is the relation between the pure consciousness realised by the sage and the 'I-am-ness' which is accepted as the primary datum of experience?

A. The undifferentiated Consciousness of pure Being is the Heart, which is what you really are. From the Heart arises the 'I-am-ness' as the primary datum of one's experience. By itself, it is completely pure in character. It is in this form of pristine purity, uncontaminated by activity and inertia, that the 'I' appears to subsist in the sage.

Q. In the sage the ego subsists in the pure form and therefore it appears as something real. Am I right?

A. The appearance of the ego in any form, either in the sage or seeker, is itself an experience. But to the seeker who is deluded into thinking that the waking state and the world are real, the ego also appears to be real. Since he sees the sage act like other individuals, he feels constrained to posit some notion of individuality with reference to the sage also.

Q. How then does the 'I'-thought, the sense of individuality function in the sage?

A. It does not function in him at all. The sage's real nature is the Heart itself because he is one and identical with the undifferentiated, Pure Consciousness referred to by the Upanishads as Supreme Consciousness. Supreme Consciousness is truly Supreme Spirit, the Absolute, and there is no Supreme Spirit other than Supreme Consciousness.

Q. Does a sage have desires?

A. The main qualities of the ordinary mind are inertia and activity; hence it is full of egoistic desires and weaknesses. But the sage's mind is pure harmony and formless, functioning in the subtle, the sheath of knowledge, through which he keeps contact with the world. His desires are therefore also pure.

Q. I am trying to understand the sage's point of view about the world. Is the world perceived after Self-realisation?

A. Why worry yourself about the world and what happens to it after Self-realisation? First, realise the Self. What does it matter if the world is perceived or not? Do you gain anything to help you in your quest by the non-perception of the world during sleep? Conversely, what would you lose now by the perception of the world? It is quite immaterial to the sage or seeker if he perceives the world or not. It is seen by both, but their viewpoints differ.

Q. If the sage and the seeker perceive the world in like manner, where is the difference between them?

A. Seeing the world, the sage sees the Self which is the substratum of all that is seen. The seeker, whether he sees the world or not, is ignorant of his true being, the Self. Take the instance of moving pictures on the screen in the cinema-show. What is there in front of you before the play begins? Merely the screen. On that screen you see the entire show, and for all appearances the pictures are real. But go and try to take hold of them. What do you take hold of? Merely the screen on which the pictures appeared. After the film, when the pictures disappear, what remains? The screen again. So with the Self. That alone exists, the pictures come and go. If you hold on to the Self, you will not be deceived by the appearance of the pictures. Nor does it matter at all if the pictures appear or disappear. Ignoring the Self the seeker thinks the world is real, just as ignoring the screen he sees merely the pictures as if they existed apart from it. If one knows that without the Seer there is nothing to be seen, just as there are no pictures without the screen, one is not deluded. The sage knows that the screen and the pictures are only the Self. With the pictures the Self is in its manifest form; without the pictures, it remains in the unmanifest form. To the sage, it is quite immaterial if the Self is in the one form or the other.

He is always the Self. But the seeker seeing the sage active gets confounded.

Q. Does Bhagavan see the world as part and parcel of himself? How does he see the world?

A. The Self alone is and nothing else. However, it is differentiated owing to ignorance.

Differentiation is threefold:

(1) of the same kind;

(2) of a different kind; and

(3) as parts in itself.

The world is not another Self that is similar to the Self. It is not different from the Self; nor is it part of the Self.

Q. Is not the world reflected on the Self?

A. For reflection, there must be an object and an image. But the Self does not admit of these differences.

Q. Does a sage have dreams?

A. Yes, he does dream, but he knows it to be a dream, in the same way as he knows the waking state to be a dream. You may call them dream no. 1 and dream no. 2. The sage being established in the fourth state – the Supreme Reality – he detachedly witnesses the three other states, waking, dreaming and dreamless sleep, as pictures superimposed on it. For those who experience waking, dream and sleep, the state of wakeful sleep, which is beyond those three states, is named the fourth. But since the fourth alone exists and since the seeming three states do not exist, know for certain that the fourth is itself that which transcends the fourth.

Q. For the sage then, there is no distinction between the three states of mind?

A. How can there be, when the mind itself is dissolved and lost in the light of Consciousness? For the sage, all the three states are equally unreal. But the seeker is unable to comprehend this, because for him the standard of reality is the waking state, whereas for the sage the standard of reality is Reality Itself. This Reality of Pure Consciousness is eternal by its nature and therefore subsists equally during what you call waking, dreaming and sleep. To him who is one with that Reality there is neither the mind nor its three states and, therefore, neither introversion nor extroversion.

His is the ever-waking state because he is awake to the eternal Self; his is the ever-dreaming state, because to him the world is no better than a repeatedly presented dream phenomenon; his is the ever-sleeping state, because he is at all times without the 'I-am-the-body' consciousness.

Q. Is there no 'I-am-the-body' idea for the sage? If, for instance, Sri Bhagavan is bitten by an insect, is there no sensation?

A. There is the sensation and there is also the idea 'I-am-the-body'. The latter is common to both sage and seeker with this difference, that the seeker thinks only the body is myself, whereas the sage knows All is of the Self, or all this is Supreme Spirit. If there be pain let it be. It is also part of the Self. The Self is perfect.

After transcending the idea 'I-am-the-body', one becomes a sage. In the absence of that idea, there cannot be either doership or doer. So a sage performs no actions. That is his experience. Otherwise, he is not a sage. However, the seeker identifies the sage with his body, which the sage does not do.

Q. I see you doing things. How can you say that you never perform actions?

A. The radio sings and speaks, but if you open it you will find no one inside. Similarly, though this body speaks like the radio, there is no one inside as a doer.

Q. I find this hard to understand. Could you please elaborate on this?

A. Various illustrations are given in books to enable us to understand how the sage can live and act without the mind, although living and acting require the use of the mind. The potter's wheel goes on turning around even after the potter has ceased to turn it because the pot is finished. In the same way, the electric fan goes on revolving for some minutes after we switch off the current. The cause and effect which created the body will make it go through whatever activities it was meant for. But the sage goes through all these activities without the notion that he is the doer of them. It is hard to understand how this is possible. The illustration generally given is that the sage performs actions in some such way as a child that is roused from sleep to eat, eats but does not remember the next morning that it ate. It has to be remembered that all these explanations are not for the sage. He knows and has no doubts. He knows that he is not the body and he knows that he is not doing anything even though his body may be engaged in some activity. These explanations are for the onlookers who think of the sage as one with a body and cannot help identifying him with his body.

Q. Is a sage capable of or likely to commit sins?

A. A seeker sees someone as a sage and identifies him with the body. Because he does not know the Self and mistakes his body for the Self, he extends the same mistake to the state of the sage. The sage is therefore considered to be the physical frame. Again since the seeker, though he is not the doer, imagines himself to be the doer and considers the actions of the body his own, he thinks the sage to be similarly acting when the body is active. But the sage himself knows the truth and is not confounded. The state of a sage cannot be determined by the seeker and therefore the question troubles only the seeker and never arises for the sage. If he is a doer he must determine the nature of the actions. The Self cannot be the doer. Find out who is the doer and the Self is revealed.

Q. So it amounts to this. To see a sage is not to understand him. You see the sage's body and not his Self-knowledge. One must, therefore, be a sage to know a sage.

A. The sage sees no one as a seeker. All are only sages in his sight. In the ignorant state, one superimposes one's ignorance on to the sage and mistakes him for a doer. In the state of Self-knowledge, the sage sees nothing separate from the Self. The Self is all-shining and only pure Self-knowledge. So there is no absence of Self-knowledge in his sight. There is an illustration for this kind of illusion or superimposition. Two friends went to sleep side by side. One of them dreamt that both of them had gone on a long journey and that they had had strange experiences. On waking up he recapitulated them and asked his friend if it was not so. The other one simply ridiculed him saying that it was only his dream and could not affect the other. So it is with the seeker who superimposes his illusory ideas on others.

Q. You have said that the sage can be and is active, and deals with men and things. I have no doubt about it now. But you say at the same time that he sees no differences; to him, all is one, he is always Consciousness. If so, how does he deal with differences, with men, with things which are surely different?

A. He sees these differences as but appearances, he sees them as not separate from the True, the Real, with which he is One.

Q. The sage seems to be more accurate in his expressions, he appreciates the differences better than the ordinary man. If sugar is sweet and wormwood is bitter to me, he too seems to realise it so. In fact, all forms, all sounds, all tastes, etc., are the same to him as they are to others. If so, how can it be said that these are mere appearances? Do they not form part of his life-experience?

A. I have said that equality is the true sign of a sage. The very term equality implies the existence of differences. It is a unity that the sage perceives in all differences, which I call equality. Equality does not mean ignorance of distinctions. When you have the Realisation you can see that these differences are very superficial, that they are not at all substantial or permanent, and what is essential in all these appearances is the One Truth, the Real. That I call Unity. You referred to sound, taste, form, smell, etc. True the sage appreciates the distinctions, but he always perceives and experiences the One Reality in all of them. That is why he has no preferences. Whether he moves about, or talks, or acts, it is all the One Reality in which he acts or moves or talks. He has nothing apart from the One Supreme Truth.

Q. They say that the sage conducts himself with absolute equality towards all?

A. Yes. Friendship, kindness, happiness and such other dispositions become natural to them. Affection towards the good, kindness towards the helpless, happiness in doing good deeds, forgiveness towards the wicked, all such things are natural characteristics of the sage. You ask about sages: they are the same in any state or condition, as they know the Reality, the Truth. In their daily routine of taking food, moving about and all the rest, they, the sages, act only for others. Not a single action is done for themselves. I have already told you many times that just as there are people whose profession is to mourn for a fee, so also the sages do things for the sake of others with detachment, without themselves being affected by them. The sage weeps with the weeping, laughs with the laughing, plays with the playful, sings with those who sing, keeping time to the song. What does he lose? His presence is like a pure, transparent mirror. It reflects the image exactly as it is. But the sage, who is only a mirror, is unaffected by actions. How can a mirror, or the stand on which it is mounted, be affected by the reflections? Nothing affects them as they are mere supports. On the other hand, the actors in the world – the doers of all acts, the seekers – must decide for themselves what song and what action is for the welfare of the world, what is in accordance with the scriptures, and what is practicable.

Q. There are said to be those liberated while still in the body and those liberated at the time of death.

A. There is no liberation. Where is the liberation?

Q. Do the scriptures not speak of liberation?

A. Liberation is synonymous with the Self. Liberation while still in the body and liberation at the time of death are all for the ignorant. The sage is not conscious of liberation or bondage. Bondage, liberation and orders of liberation are all said for a seeker in order that ignorance might be shaken off. There is only Liberation and nothing else.

Q. It is all right from the standpoint of Bhagavan. But what about us?

A. The difference 'he' and 'I' are the obstacles to Self-knowledge.

Q. An Indian philosopher, in one of his books, interpreting Sankara, says that there is no such thing as liberation at the time of death, for after death, one takes a body of light in which one remains till the whole of humanity becomes liberated.

A. That cannot be Sankara's view. In verse 566 of Vivekachudamani he says that after the dissolution of the physical sheath the liberated man becomes like "water poured into water and oil into oil". It is a state in which there is neither bondage nor liberation. Taking another body means throwing a veil, however subtle, upon reality, which is bondage. Liberation is Absolute and irrevocable.

Q. How can we say the sage is not in two planes? He moves about with us in the world and sees the various objects we see. It is not as if he does not see them. For instance, he walks along. He sees the path he is treading. Suppose there is a chair or table placed across that path; he sees it, avoids it and goes around. So, have we not to admit he sees the world and the objects there, while of course, he sees the Self?

A. You say the sage sees the path, treads it, comes across obstacles, avoids them, etc. In whose eyesight is all this, in the sage's or yours? He sees only the Self and all in the Self.

Q. Are there not illustrations given in our books to explain this natural state clearly to us?

A. There are. For instance, you see a reflection in the mirror and the mirror. You know the mirror to be the reality and the picture in it a mere reflection. Is it necessary that to see the mirror we should cease to see the reflection in it?

Q. What are the fundamental tests for discovering men of great spirituality, since some are reported to behave like insane people?

A. The sage's mind is known only to the sage. One must be a sage oneself in order to understand another sage. However, the peace of mind which permeates the saint's atmosphere is the only means by which the seeker understands the greatness of the saint.

His words or actions or appearance are no indication of his greatness, for they are ordinarily beyond the comprehension of common people.

Q. Why is it said in scriptures that the sage is like a child?

A. A child and a sage are similar in a way. Incidents interest a child only so long as they last. It ceases to think of them after they have passed away. So then, it is apparent that they do not leave any impression on the child and it is not affected by them mentally. So it is with a sage.

Q. You are Bhagavan. So you should know when I shall get Self-knowledge. Tell me when I shall be a sage.

A. If I am Bhagavan there is no one besides the Self – therefore no sage or seeker. If otherwise, I am as good as you are and know as much as yourself. Either way, I cannot answer your question.

Coming here, some people do not ask about themselves. They ask: "Does the liberated soul see the world? Is he affected by past actions? What is liberation after being disembodied? Is one liberated only after being disembodied or even while alive in the body? Should the body of the sage resolve itself in light or disappear from view in any other manner? Can he be liberated though the body is left behind as a corpse?" Their questions are endless. Why worry oneself in so many ways? Does liberation consist in knowing these things? Therefore I say to them, "Leave liberation alone. Is there bondage? Know this. See yourself first and foremost."

The One Thing to Resolve All Doubts

Q. What is that one thing, knowing which all doubts are resolved?

A. Know the doubter. If the doubter is held, the doubts will not arise. Here the doubter is transcendent. Again when the doubter ceases to exist, there will be no doubts arising. From where will they arise? All are sages, liberated souls. Only they are not aware of the fact. Doubts must be uprooted. This means that the doubter must be uprooted. Here the doubter is the mind.

Q. What is the method?

A. 'Who am I?' is the investigation.

References & Acknowledgements

I would like to acknowledge and thank the original sources of the material used in this book. Please refer to them for a fuller understanding of the subject:

"I had read no books..." – *Self Realization* by B.V. Narasimha Swami, Ch. 5

"These readings from the Ribhu Gita..." – *Self Realization*, B.V. Narasimha Swami, Ch. 26

"It doesn't matter..." – *The Mountain Path*, June 1993, p. 103

A story of Ribhu and Nidagha: – *Letters from Sri Ramanasramam*, 25th April 1948

Selections from the *Ribhu Gita* were revised and adapted from *The Mountain Path*, Volume 9, Numbers 1 and 2, 1972

Questions and answers were revised and adapted from:
– *Talks with Sri Ramana Maharshi*
– *Be As You Are: The Teachings of Sri Ramana Maharshi*, Edited by David Godman

This book owes its existence to a long out-of-print book from the 1970s called *The Heart of the Ribhu Gita* by Franklin Jones, and has grown out of the need to once again make this great work more accessible to the public.

I would like to say a personal 'Thank you' to Stephen Gawtry for patiently bearing and responding to my constant requests for help and to Michael Mann for believing in this book and persevering in that belief.

Also, to all those at O-Books that have helped correct, design, and print this book and bring it to the world.

Finally, I would like to thank Sri Ramanasramam for giving me permission to use the words of Bhagavan Sri Ramana Maharshi as well as for their ongoing work in spreading his teachings.

MANTRA
BOOKS

EASTERN RELIGION & PHILOSOPHY

We publish books on Eastern religions and philosophies. Books
that aim to inform and explore the various traditions that began in
the East and have migrated West.
If you have enjoyed this book, why not tell other readers by
posting a review on your preferred book site. Recent bestsellers
from MANTRA BOOKS are:

The Way Things Are
A Living Approach to Buddhism
Lama Ole Nydahl
An introduction to the teachings of the Buddha, and how to make
use of these teachings in everyday life.
Paperback: 978-1-84694-042-2 ebook: 978-1-78099-845-9

Back to the Truth
5000 Years of Advaita
Dennis Waite
A demystifying guide to Advaita for both those new to, and those
familiar with this ancient, non-dualist philosophy from India.
Paperback: 978-1-90504-761-1 ebook: 978-184694-624-0

Shinto: A celebration of Life
Aidan Rankin
Introducing a gentle but powerful spiritual pathway reconnecting
humanity with Great Nature and affirming all aspects of life.
Paperback: 978-1-84694-438-3 ebook: 978-1-84694-738-4

In the Light of Meditation
Mike George
A comprehensive introduction to the practice of meditation and the spiritual principles behind it. A 10 lesson meditation programme with CD and internet support.
Paperback: 978-1-90381-661-5

The Less Dust the More Trust
Participating in The Shamatha Project, Meditation and Science
Adeline van Waning, MD PhD
The inside-story of a woman participating in frontline meditation research, exploring the interfaces of mind-practice, science and psychology.
Paperback: 978-1-78099-948-7 ebook: 978-1-78279-657-2

I Know How To Live, I Know How To Die
The Teachings of Dadi Janki: A warm, radical, and life-affirming view of who we are, where we come from, and what time is calling us to do
Neville Hodgkinson
Life and death are explored in the context of frontier science and deep soul awareness.
Paperback: 978-1-78535-013-9 ebook: 978-1-78535-014-6

Living Jainism
An Ethical Science
Aidan Rankin, Kanti V. Mardia
A radical new perspective on science rooted in intuitive awareness and deductive reasoning.
Paperback: 978-1-78099-912-8 ebook: 978-1-78099-911-1

A Path of Joy
Popping into Freedom
Paramananda Ishaya
A simple and joyful path to spiritual enlightenment.
Paperback: 978-1-78279-323-6 ebook: 978-1-78279-322-9

Ordinary Women, Extraordinary Wisdom
The Feminine Face of Awakening
Rita Marie Robinson
A collection of intimate conversations with female spiritual
teachers who live like ordinary women, but are engaged with their
true natures.
Paperback: 978-1-84694-068-2 ebook: 978-1-78099-908-1

The Way of Nothing
Nothing in the Way
Paramananda Ishaya
A fresh and light-hearted exploration of the amazing reality of
nothingness.
Paperback: 978-1-78279-307-6 ebook: 978-1-78099-840-4

Readers of ebooks can buy or view any of these bestsellers by
clicking on the live link in the title. Most titles are published in
paperback and as an ebook. Paperbacks are available in traditional
bookshops. Both print and ebook formats are available online.

Find more titles and sign up to our readers' newsletter at
http://www.johnhuntpublishing.com/mind-body-spirit.
Follow us on Facebook at https://www.facebook.com/OBooks
and Twitter at https://twitter.com/obooks.